REASONS (NOT) TO DANCE

José Angel Araguz

FUTURECYCLE PRESS
www.futurecycle.org

Copyright © 2015 José Angel Araguz
All Rights Reserved

Published by FutureCycle Press
Lexington, Kentucky, USA

ISBN 978-1-938853-87-6

for ani, my co-conspirator

Contents

First Night..7
The One Left Behind...8
Clams...9
Oceans...10
Relinquished...11
The Nun's Lament...12
Field Mouse...13
Pinky...14
Extreme Home Makeover (the Mother)..................................15
On Waiting to Hear from a Job Application...........................16
Ink...17
Tesla..18
Wild Flight..19
After a Taoist Proverb..20
The Ashtray...21
Instead of a Postcard..22
Clock Ode...23
Doppelganger..24
Wisp..25
Lucky God..26
Twitch...27
Eve..28
Spinster...29
Intimacy: a sequence..30
Blindness...31
Lovers..32
Dictionary...33
What He Means by Desire...34
Hangman Ode...35
Look..36
Making the Days...37
Rewarded..38
Acknowledgments

First Night

No one recalls their first night on earth, night like all others, with words and darkness, cries and stars, only you didn't try to fight or count them all. No part of you recalls because no part of you reached out. You at your most hidden, unknowing but known, fresh, a secret shared for the first time. Like all things secret, you quickly lost track of where you came from. Darkness and words, cries and stars—none of it feels new anymore.

The One Left Behind

As the Pied Piper led them off into the hill, there was one child who didn't follow the rest. Born with one leg shorter, he hobbled to his own heartbeat, but found it wasn't strong enough to keep with the others. The other children became noise, specks, a memory, the silence of what became his life. The street the child was left on is now kept vacant. Like all cursed places, there is a marker telling what happened. There is no mention of the one left behind. Later, there were those in the village who recalled there being an innkeeper who'd always grow angry whenever travelers went on too long telling a story, who'd interrupt and say: *When one makes a long trip, they bring back something to talk about. Do that. Shut up and take this with you.*

Clams

Clams open and close to the rhythm of the tides they live in, and continue to do so when transported to other water. Once, New Jersey clams were taken to Ohio where they kept their rhythm to New Jersey tides, until one day they stopped opening. A few days later, they began to open and close again in the rhythm of the tides of Ohio—if Ohio had an ocean, that is.

Oceans

The oceans have not always been here. First, there was a man who grew up feeling out of place, who felt a pain he could not name and could do nothing about. He thought it could be love, for he had seen love acted out in others, but when he looked at the faces he knew, he did not see love. One night, he had a dream where the moon talked to him, called him to sit with her. When he said he could not, she turned away slowly, and he entered a darkness that woke him up crying, unable to move. The man kept crying for days, his tears drawing up around him, lifting him, and when he felt himself rise, he decided to keep on until he made the moon come back, and she did, slowly. The oceans have not always been here. First there was a man. Then there was sorrow.

Relinquished

after Lafcadio Hearn

A Buddhist priest, upon receiving a note of love from a woman who had seen him only in passing and could not think of anything else and now hoped for a response from his heart, wrote a letter himself saying that he relinquished his body for he was growing weak and did not want to sin and sent it to his superior before heading out in the darkness in time to kneel in between the rails as an oncoming train made its scheduled trail of smoke and sound in the night leaving what was left of the man's heart to be turned over and over in the sleepless thoughts of a woman.

The Nun's Lament

after Judith Ortiz Cofer

One night, I saw the figure of a man making his way towards my window. I had been looking across the roof of the chapel, stark in white moonlight. I closed my eyes, stood still, how long, I cannot say. The figure of the man, there behind my eyelids, flashed from shadow arms swinging, clambering across the roof, to a shadow flock of birds stirring in the air in unison, all but one taking off away from me. The one shot straight to me, past me, left me heavy, my pulse beating like wings inside. What I heard was not coming closer, was not hurting me, what I heard was restless. I had become a cloister for the heart, a space where the heart waited, idle, mid-flight. When I opened my eyes, there was the roof, clear, and a train in the distance, its whistle bursting.

Field Mouse

For the black owl, the one hardest to see at night, his whole body is an eye. There are those who think he is inventing problems. How could one invent the black owl, he wonders. You would misplace it as soon as you began to count out feathers, black against black against black. Misplace the talons. Misplace the beak. How could one be so foolish? It is too much work. He makes out the first of the stars in silence and braces for the rest.

Pinky

Like a girl, says my uncle about the way I hold my coffee, my small finger hooked in a J. Cool as I can, I tell him what I heard: a king once demanded silence throughout his palace, had everyone grow out their pinky nails. Knocking was banned. Doors were scratched by hands curled almost to fists. A kingdom of whispers. People scared white as the powder edging their faces. Smiling, he shoves his shovel-sharp nail into the air and makes a sound behind his teeth that could be a laugh or a pebble struck against a pane of glass.

Extreme Home Makeover (the Mother)

Weeks now since the cameras crowed over each step and boom mikes swept up words like crumbs, she still looks over her shoulder for shadows to tell her where to stand. The kids still practice waking up, shifting in their beds, waiting for cues.

Not finding him in the house, she goes out to the garage to find her husband asleep in his truck like he did when their old place was not their place but a hole in the ground. In the dark, she can only make out half of his face swaying with his slow breathing, each breath bringing to focus what could be ash in his beard.

On Waiting to Hear from a Job Application

This wide coast I pace with my breath cut close to my teeth. Such is the awe and openness of my days, anything could claw its way out of the waves, anything could arrive and make this silence give.

Ink

One is told to use only black when filling out papers for work or those about one's vital information.

One can then imagine hand after hand in all colors writing on sidewalks and tables and sand.

These are not serious hands.

These words are not real words.

Tesla

Whenever a newspaper is left on his bench or is carried his way on the wind, he punches it away. Which is where I found him today: standing his ground against a pale, flittering ghost made of words that he raps at, knocking on a door perhaps answered in some other world where a storm threatens in sudden, far-off thunder.

Wild Flight

Having walked in on the man shaving his face in the men's room at the park, he stops, feels he should turn away, but then notices the others standing at their business, their backs to this act of clearing some of the coarseness of the body, and before he can feel any more out of place he looks back to find the man different, his hands cupped before him holding what could be a bird made of light that rises and takes wild flight against him, into him.

After a Taoist Proverb

For the blind man, there is no night, only a break in time, a scaling back of the noise around him, a hand pulling the sounds around him as he does a blanket as it begins to grow colder.

Ask him to describe the sun, and he says it is a fire holding conversation with everyone.

The moon is him alone with his heart.

The Ashtray

One can imagine a nightclub by this name, rooms where shadows crowd and push dim faces into dim thoughts, where glass and ice rattle and shine with a light as fevered and uncaught as that of fireflies one can make out blearily through the dark, small sparks that singe, burn, and snuff themselves out.

Instead of a Postcard

for N. S.

Friends: I apologize for addressing you all at once like this, and for not calling or writing a letter. Remember, talking: that's what the bars are for. If you don't hear from me it is because of a conversation I am having either with myself or some streetlamp of a man, posted in his ways every night. I have moved; you may guess where, and how, and tell me what life you would have me lead. Some follow their hearts; I follow the moon. Allow me my phases and you will have your tides. I write tonight not to tell you of a new city but to share what the new city would say of me, and seeing as I do not speak the language of cities, I send this image as proof that part of me is yet alive: a smile, a dress, the light rising off the back of a hand covering my eyes.

Clock Ode

The face of the clock is the house where time lives.

You tell time, time does not answer back: like a cloud that by being shaped forgets itself.

The clock holds still, indifferent to its meddling moustache.

Death will not come wielding a scythe but a clock: you'll be caught working out the math of the sudden hour.

Dust gathers on the face of the clock: crowds struck by the way these hands keep moving.

The face of the clock: shield of the antihero, marks on the surface tell the story of what one is losing.

An ant crawls across blank paper on the table; you worry the minutes have fallen.

Doppelganger

Neither being forgotten nor reviled unjustly after dying should plague the writer's mind, but being talked about by people who have never read their books and so to be invoked in words unfamiliar and unchosen, words not one's own but following one's name, recreating and strangering it, so that someone who never existed comes into being and takes the place of a particular hand and heart and mouth—this, this is to be feared.

Wisp

When I pointed out the white wisp on my fingernail as a child, my aunt told me these things appeared to mark one's sins.

Later, when I was told it was due to a deficiency of sorts, I said: *I know.*

Lucky God

I know others have seen the god who looks like me by the way they play cat when they see me: the refusal to make eye contact, the turning away in the opposite direction or the walking right past me as if they had already left their scent on me. For a minor god, for he must be, he gets around. Lucky god. So many pass without seeing me, I could be a wall. So many pass, self-satisfied, I know they have met him in a paper bag or a stray ice cube on the floor. When I do find myself in conversation, it is small talk, palaver, and I am reassured of my penance: to placate and play along with the god-forsaken.

Twitch

There is the story of the man who swallowed a fly and often found himself telling the tale: each time the story would bring the buzz into his throat, the legs and wings working, the muscles of his breath taking in a creature that comes back in the words he keeps finding reasons to share.

Eve

And what if there was not a snake anywhere in that garden where she went walking, passing by the tree of knowledge and stopping as she did twice a day, at morning and at dusk, so that it was the first and last thing she thought of each day, so much time spent idly staring out at the perfect apples, bright and round as small red suns, that hung there on black branches, half-hidden apples in the shadow of leaves, the leaves themselves dark compared to that fruit forbidden her who stood there one day gazing as if at a reflection and feeling something she could not name only stood there with her mouth half-open as a breeze eased past her and shook the branches enough so that one apple fell down, and before she knew what she was doing Eve had her reason and knew it all.

Spinster

You want me to tell you about life here. There was a castle where a woman was buried within a wall as a sacrifice. They knew nothing about her except she loved to dance. Later, there was a law against dancing. You knew when someone was breaking the law because the castle would begin to shake. Mother called the woman a saint: only someone who was pure could root out those who wronged. The night my father left, the castle crumbled down. Granted, this is only partly true. It was told to me and I tell you, not because I believe in dancing castles. I believe you have come here wanting stories, and all I have learned are reasons not to dance.

Intimacy: a sequence

(Matchstick)—She says it as an insult about a woman walking by, and I wonder what is stuck between her teeth and the woman's sunlit hair flashing across her eyes.

(Vanity)—*On a good day I don't notice my face,* she says, with a look in her eyes full of that glassy sheen of magazines too busy with the stars.

(In the Bath)—*This would be better,* she says, *if you were a woman,* and then flicks her cigarette, sending ash to scatter and sink into my reflection.

(Brown)—She tells me brown is not a real color, that the art teacher told her brown is an aberration, a mistake of the eyes. I move to say something but everything I come up with feels wrong, and so I remain silent, her eyes still on me with a look I now feel is trying to correct me.

(Intimacy)—She told me once that what she sees in a mirror is often not a reflection but more a fear that she may only be colors lingering.

(God)—*God is in the rain,* she says, then turns to cross the street, making her way against this sudden traffic of blue light.

Blindness

A woman catches him staring at her and he turns, walks in the opposite direction, thinking: *I am used to and at times even enjoy a woman walking away from me. My sight dances, catches on the wind like a paper bag restlessly turning over on itself; this is how I feel—a piece of trash, happily a piece of trash.*

Speaking of their past, about loneliness and need, she asks him if he masturbates and he dismisses it quickly as a bad habit, like chewing one's fingernails or smoking, says he feels ashamed each time afterwards, and she later wonders if the same hand running down her side as they settle into bed will one day wish to unlearn her too.

What is to become of me here whittling time in a fist?

The joke is he could go blind from this, not from the staring, but from the act at the culmination of the staring, which, of course, seems unlikely, but still, when he finishes, he lies in the dark and thinks about this and wishes for the blossoming colors to cease, only to catch himself distracted, having to wish again.

Lovers

I had wanted to ask her if I was anything like the man she was leaving or if she thought herself anything like the woman I had left and if so I could assure her that she was not but never got around to asking or if I had she never had a chance to answer so busy were we with each other we rarely had time for answers but were left with questions unasked and reworded in the light of the other's eyes.

Dictionary

Paging through the dictionary, looking for the names of things, he imagines each definition as a recipe, words collected and waiting to be brought together into that taste singular to the human mind—meaning—a thing that, as he reads, he savors, and as he savors, wants more.

What He Means by Desire

Something of the wolf who hunted only during the day, thinking he'd be unable to see in the dark—who struggled for food straight into the evening, then was struck by the light swelling in the black—who fell in love when he looked up and saw the moon, a thing he had never seen before—who proceeded to go hungry—who spent the rest of his nights gazing past the stars, pining so much he could not help the howls he heard himself croak—who pitched everything he was to the sky, thinking the moon had ears, thinking she might come down and fill his body with the light shooting through the darkness, claiming him, making him fierce, restless, alive—who felt whetted by hunger, more and more of him giving way as more and more of the moon gave way—who, when in the dark, when unable to see, when each breath felt sickled on his tongue, began to remember he had to hunt, he was animal, he was a struggle he could no longer ignore—

Hangman Ode

Each wrong guess draws out a man whose life depends on how fast the words are figured out.

The goal is to figure out the words correctly and leave little of the dying man exposed.

When the little man is complete, he dies.

When you lose, the words remain unfinished, broken with gaps—footprints where something has been let to walk away.

Look

after Kafka

When the afternoon light has turned to evening light and she turns to tell you this, points out the purple as the kind of purple she would want a whole room painted in, and you consider what that room would be like if you stood in it, this purple at every side, when the sky you are both looking at seems different each time you look and in your mind say *look* to yourself and look because she has been looking and wants you to as well, when she perhaps has even gone as far as to enter that room and close the door behind her and is standing alone with this purple at every side, when all you can do is turn from the purple glints across her eyes and look again at the sky, a deeper purple now that imbues itself on the stones of the church, on the sides of the tree, on the slick of the leaves, on the skin of the couple passing by, a purple distance between them, a purple silence and a purple expression on each of their faces—then it is time to shut the blinds and for a moment stand with her in the completely darkened room and let your eyes and hers adjust.

Making the Days

The people who make the days assign each person the steps they must walk, the breaths to be taken. Much of their job is movement. On some days, they take their time. After the dull work of picking the TV shows, the lines to be waited in, and the number of birds to fly over the head of someone walking down a dirt road, they sit back and take in what it might mean, the day almost completed before them. Perhaps the person in charge of the dust looks to the one in charge of tears with a look of sympathy. The person in charge of sweat looks down at his hands and finds them empty. Maybe one is proud of each current in a river, another proud of each bowl made under the hand of someone who thinks oneself at one with wet clay. These are the days when one feels different, not that time has stopped but that it goes on in a different way, like rain running down into the ocean and disappearing. These are the days when you look up on your walk home and notice how big the tree on the corner really is, how wide, how alive and green, how talkative with the wind moving every branch, every leaf. And some thought enters your mind about how every leaf is moving, and inside each leaf something else moves and, inside of that, even more movement. And so on. And you wait there until you remember that you yourself were in the middle of moving—and then begin to do so.

Rewarded

Showering under a low faucet, I see the sun begin to show at the window. The room fills with orange light, and I am like the man rewarded for his silence as he slept under an orange tree that dropped its blossoms over him in such a way he heard a voice thank him for his words on emptiness. When he spoke up and said he had said nothing, the tree agreed he had said nothing, and the tree had heard nothing, and the rush of blossoms poured on.

Acknowledgments

Special thanks to the editors of the following publications where the pieces noted were published (at times in earlier versions):

Cider Press Review: "Instead of a Postcard"
The Citron Review: "Twitch"
The Fox Chase Review: "After a Taoist Proverb"
The Inflectionist Review: "First Night"
The Laurel Review: "Field Mouse," "Clock Ode," "Lucky God"
NANO Fiction: "Pinky"
Pretty Owl Poetry: "Oceans," "Spinster"
The Prose Poem Project: "On Waiting to Hear from a Job Application," "Eve"
RHINO Poetry: "The Ashtray"
Right Hand Pointing: "Ink"
Star 82 Review: "Clams," "Wisp," "(Brown)"
Stirring: a literary collection: "Intimacy: a sequence" (excerpts)
Things in Light: "Extreme Home Makeover (the mother)"
Washington Square Review: "Wild Flight"
White Stag: "Tesla"

The pieces "Relinquished" and "Look" won second place in *Blue Earth Review*'s 2014 Flash Fiction Contest.

Cover artwork and author photo by Andrea Schreiber; cover and interior book design by Diane Kistner; Adobe Garamond Pro text with Dimitrina titling

About FutureCycle Press

FutureCycle Press is dedicated to publishing lasting English-language poetry books, chapbooks, and anthologies in both print-on-demand and ebook formats. Founded in 2007 by long-time independent editor/publishers and partners Diane Kistner and Robert S. King, the press incorporated as a nonprofit in 2012. A number of our editors are distinguished poets and writers in their own right, and we have been actively involved in the small press movement going back to the early seventies.

The FutureCycle Poetry Book Prize and honorarium is awarded annually for the best full-length volume of poetry we publish in a calendar year. Introduced in 2013, our Good Works projects are anthologies devoted to issues of universal significance, with all proceeds donated to a related worthy cause. Our Selected Poems series highlights contemporary poets with a substantial body of work to their credit; with this series we strive to resurrect work that has had limited distribution and is now out of print.

We are dedicated to giving all of the authors we publish the care their work deserves, making our catalog of titles the most diverse and distinguished it can be, and paying forward any earnings to fund more great books.

Over the years, we've learned a few things about independent publishing. We've also evolved a unique, resilient publishing model that allows us to focus mainly on vetting and preserving for posterity the most books of exceptional quality without becoming overwhelmed with bookkeeping and mailing, fund-raising activities, or taxing editorial and production "bubbles." To find out more about what we are doing, come see us at www.futurecycle.org.

Made in the USA
Middletown, DE
03 July 2015